T0020602

THE LITTLE BOOK OF
KINGS
& QUEENS

Published in 2022 by OH!
An Imprint of Welbeck Non-Fiction Limited,
part of Welbeck Publishing Group.
Based in London and Sydney.
www.welbeckpublishing.com

ISBN 978-1-80069-179-7

Compiled and written by: RH
Project manager: Russell Porter
Production: Jess Brisley

A CIP catalogue record for this book is available from the British Library

Printed in China

10 9 8 7 6 5 4 3 2 1

Illustrations: Shutterstock.com

THE LITTLE BOOK OF
KINGS & QUEENS

A JEWELLED COLLECTION OF ROYAL WIT & WISDOM

CONTENTS

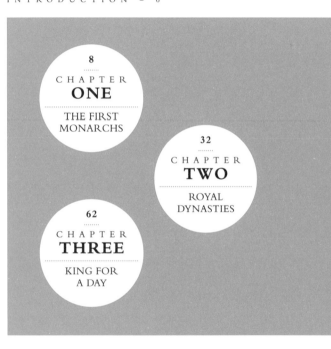

INTRODUCTION

Kings, queens and monarchs of many other varieties are still present in a whole host of countries around the world, thousands of years after the first rulers took charge, and despite the fact that many of them hold no power. However, the vast majority of the world has no monarchy and so is always interested to see what those unelected representatives and leaders get up to elsewhere.

A few countries managed to get rid of their royal families hundreds of years ago, some got shot of them temporarily before then letting them back in again, and others "freed" themselves while allowing a figurehead to stay – but with no sovereign power.

Kings and queens have been of interest to pretty much all of us for as long as we can remember, and it's not really a surprise why. Holding on to power has all too often come at a great cost, with revolutions and wars in some places, and stresses and strains in most. But some countries have made it to the twenty-first century with a figurehead they are still proud of, one who is loved by the people and who commands respect, does great work and is famous the world over. We hear about a few of them in this book, as well as kings, queens, princes, princesses, emperors and empresses from throughout history.

Some rulers were born to power, some were bred and some seized it by force. *The Little Guide to Kings and Queens* is right royally filled up with fascinating quotes, sayings and mottoes, as well as intriguing facts, witty and wise quips and a few diverting lists.

It adds up to a regal reserve of recreation for your mind: enjoy thyself, subject!

CHAPTER
ONE

The First Monarchs

The earliest recorded
monarchs ruled in Sumer and
Egypt, around 3000 BCE.
This chapter touches upon
some of the first kings and
queens to wield power.

> **"C**onquering the world on horseback is easy; it is dismounting and governing that is hard.**"**

Genghis Khan

Circa 1155–1227 CE

"**B**efore God, a king is as great a sinner as his meanest subject."

Frederick the Great
(1712–1786)

Jadwiga (Hedwig),
the first female monarch
of Poland, was crowned as
Rex Poloniae
– King of Poland –
in 1384.

"Too many kings can ruin an army."

Homer
(Circa 700 BCE)

"Kubaba gave bread to the fisherman and gave water, she made him offer the fish to Esagila. Marduk, the king, the prince of the Apsû, favoured her and said, 'Let it be so!' He entrusted to Kubaba, the tavern-keeper, sovereignty over the whole world."

The Weidner Chronicle
Ancient Babylonian text

The first female ruler in
recorded history was
Kubaba, Queen of Sumer,
around 2400 BCE

"You have power over your mind – not outside events. Realize this, and you will find strength.**"**

Marcus Aurelius
Roman emperor (120–180 CE)

"Until the kings become philosophers, there will be no end to the troubles of the states."

Plato

The Republic, *circa 375 BCE*

Oldest Royal Families

Kingdom of **Sweden**, founded circa 970 CE

Kingdom of **Denmark**, founded circa 935 CE

Kingdom of **Norway**, founded circa 885 CE

British Monarchy, founded 871 CE

Kingdom of **Morocco**, founded 788 CE

Sultanate of **Oman**, founded 751 CE
(as an Imamate, current Sultanate established 1749 CE)

Kingdom of **Cambodia**, founded 68 CE

Imperial House of **Japan**, founded 660 BCE

"It is not until the end of the Middle Kingdom that we find, for the first time, clear evidence for a female king of Egypt. Her name was Sobekneferu … The name means, 'The beauties of Sobek', the crocodile god.**"**

Jimmy Dunn
"Sobekneferu: The First Certain Female King of Egypt"

"Think of how many of us are fighting, and why. Then you will win this battle or die. That is what I, a woman, plan to do. Let the men live as slaves if they want. I won't!"

Boudicca

Pre-battle speech, circa 60 CE

Boudicca

was a Celtic queen who led a rebellion against the Romans in England.

Initially successful, her army razed Colchester, St Albans and London, around 60 CE but she was eventually defeated.

"**M**ake haste slowly."

Caesar Augustus

The first Roman emperor (63 BCE –14 CE)

"Monarchy is the one system of government where power is exercised for the good of all."

Aristotle

(384–322 BCE)

The earliest known
ruler of Macedonia was
Alexander I, who ruled from
498 to 454 BCE.

Alexander the Great
was Alexander III, who ruled
from 336 to 323 BCE.

"There is nothing impossible
to him who will try."

Alexander the Great
(356–323 BCE)

"**B**ut because I do it with a small ship, I am called a pirate, whilst you, who do it with a great fleet, you are an emperor."

Saint Augustine
The City of God, *426 CE*

According to legend, the Imperial House of Japan was founded in 660 BCE by Japan's first emperor, Jimmu, making it the oldest continuous hereditary monarchy in the world.

Although Japan's monarchy has mythological origins, the country recognizes 11 February, 660 BCE as the official date of its founding.

Charlemagne (748–814 CE) ruled as King of the Franks, King of the Lombards and Emperor of the Carolingian Empire at different time periods. He had a major impact during the early Middle Ages as he went about uniting the majority of central and western Europe, for which he is called the "Father of Europe".

"**A** man should either not converse with kings at all, or say what is agreeable to them."

Aesop
(620–564 BCE)

"**W**ise kings have generally wise counsellors, as he must be a wise man himself who is capable of distinguishing one."

Diogenes
(Circa 404–323 BCE)

The king
can do no wrong.

Latin proverb

CHAPTER
TWO

Royal Dynasties

While many monarchies have died away, there are still 28 royal families around the world. This chapter takes a look at some of them…

"**P**ublic office must not be a means to profit or become rich."

King Felipe VI of Spain
(1968–)

"May Allah guide us to the good of the kingdom of Bahrain and its loyal people."

Hamad bin Isa Al Khalifa

(1950–)

"**I**t is not always easy to say where we are from, what nationality we are. Home is where our heart is – and that cannot always be confined within national borders."

King Harald V of Norway
Welcome speech, 2016

Royal Families of the World

Principality of **Andorra**

Kingdom of **Bahrain**, House of Al Khalifa

Kingdom of **Belgium**,
House of Saxe-Coburg and Gotha

Kingdom of **Bhutan**, House of Wangchuck

Brunei Darussalam, House of Bolkiah

Kingdom of **Cambodia**,
House of Norodom

Kingdom of **Denmark**,
House of Glücksburg

Kingdom of **Eswatini**, House of Dlamini

Japan, House of Yamato

ROYAL DYNASTIES

Hashemite Kingdom of **Jordan**,
House of Hashim

State of **Kuwait**, House of Al Sabah

Kingdom of **Lesotho**, House of Moshesh

Principality of **Liechtenstein**,
House of Liechtenstein

Grand Duchy of **Luxembourg**,
House of Luxembourg-Nassau

Malaysia, House of Pahang

Principality of **Monaco**, House of Grimaldi

Kingdom of **Morocco**, House of Alawi

Kingdom of the **Netherlands**,
House of Orange-Nassau

Kingdom of **Norway**, House of Glücksburg

Sultanate of **Oman**, House of Al Said

State of **Qatar**, House of Al Thani

Kingdom of **Saudi Arabia**,
House of Saud

Kingdom of **Spain**,
House of Bourbon–Anjou

Kingdom of **Sweden**, House of Bernadotte

Kingdom of **Thailand**, House of Chakri

Kingdom of **Tonga**, House of Tupou

United Arab Emirates,
House of Al Nahyan

United Kingdom (and other
Commonwealth realms), House of Windsor

"**Q**ueen Paola and I will never forget the ties that have grown between the people and us during the course of the years. Thank you for your confidence, tokens of sympathy and support, sometimes even with a little criticism. We always loved you."

King Albert II of Belgium

After announcing his abdication due to ill health in 2013

"As a small country, both in size and population, our future hinges on the quality of our people."

Hassanal Bolkiah, Sultan of Brunei
(1946–)

Eswatini (formerly Swaziland)
is an absolute monarchy.
The head of state is the
king (Ngwenyama), who by
tradition reigns along with
his mother (Ndlovukati).

"I sincerely hope for the happiness of the people and further progress of the country, and for world peace.**"**

Emperor Naruhito of Japan
(1960–)

"**W**e should face reality and our past mistakes in an honest, adult way. Boasting of glory does not make glory, and singing in the dark does not dispel fear."

King Hussein of Jordan

The Essential Worldwide Laws of Life

by Sir John Templeton, 2012

"One learns from the past and learns about it for the future.**"**

Sheikh Sabar Al-Ahmed Al-Jaber Al-Sabar

(1929–2020)

45

"This year's Liechtenstein celebration is enough, with the celebration of the 300th anniversary of the principality.**"**

Prince Hans–Adam II of Liechtenstein

On rejecting celebrations of his jubilee, 2019

"Recent events show us, however, that stability and peace on our continent are not permanent institutions. Quite the opposite."

Henri, Grand Duke of Luxembourg
(1945–)

Malaysia is the only country
in the world to have a rotational
monarchy, in place since the
country became independent
in 1957.

The top job is passed between
nine hereditary state rulers, with
a rotation happening once every
five years.

"She was always present and ready to do things either with me or for me if I couldn't do them. Let's say the change is that we worked as a team and the team has been split up."

Prince Rainier III of Monaco

(1923–2005)

On his late wife, Grace Kelly

"My childhood was very sheltered. I grew up in a palace. But I lived in Morocco as a Moroccan citizen.**"**

King Mohammed VI of Morocco
Interview in Time, *2000*

"I want to be a traditional king first and foremost, building on the tradition of my predecessors standing for continuity and stability in this country, but also a 21st-century king who can unite, represent and encourage society."

King Willem-Alexander of the Netherlands
National Post, *2013*

Japan

is currently the only
remaining nation to have an
emperor as monarch.

“In the Sultanate of Oman, we must purify ourselves. We must not fall sick and then seek treatment; we must apply the doctrine of prevention is better than cure.”

Sultan Qaboos bin Said
(1940–2020)

"I will be father to the young, brother to the elderly. I am but one of you; whatever troubles you, troubles me; whatever pleases you, pleases me."

King Fahd bin Abdulaziz Al Saud of Saudi Arabia

(1921–2005)

"The crown must constantly earn citizens' appreciation, respect and trust.**"**

King Felipe VI of Spain
(1968–)

"I have been king for 38 years, for which I am very proud, and during those many years I have felt a strong support from the Swedish people.**"**

King Carl XVI Gustaf of Sweden
(1946–)

"Learning is a never-ending process. Those who wish to advance in their work must constantly seek more knowledge."

King Bhumibol the Great of Thailand
(1927–2016)

"The race for excellence has no finish line."

Sheikh Mohammed bin Rashid
Al Maktoum, Ruler of the Emirate of Dubai
(1949–)

Andorra is the world's
only co-principality: one
prince is the President
of France, the other Bishop
of Urgell.

The princes must exercise
their authority together.

The British royal family
controls nearly
$28bn in assets, including
the Crown Estate ($19.5bn),
Buckingham Palace
($4.98bn) and the Duchy of
Cornwall ($1.3bn).

Source: forbes.com

"There is a Cambodian proverb which says, 'While you are eating fruit, don't forget who planted it.' We must not forget our king and his vital role in securing a victory for democracy in our country."

Hun Sen,
Prime Minister of Cambodia
(1952–)

CHAPTER

THREE

King
for a Day

Throughout history,
famous (and infamous) kings,
queens, princes, princesses,
emperors – and more – have
made their mark on
the world...

The Longest-Reigning Monarchs in History

Sobhuza II, Swaziland (Eswatini) – 82 years
Louis XIV, France – 72 years
Johann II, Liechtenstein – 70 years
Bhumibol Adulyadej – 70 years
Elizabeth II, United Kingdom – 69 years⋆
K'inich Janaab'Pakal, Maya – 68 years
Franz Joseph I, Austrian Empire – 67 years
Constantine VIII, Byzantine Empire – 66 years
Basil II, Byzantine Empire, 65 years
Victoria, United Kingdom – 63 years

⋆ Still counting as of November 2021

"It is better to inspire a reform than to enforce it."

Queen Catherine the Great
(1729–1796)

The Current
Longest-Reigning Monarchs

Elizabeth II, **United Kingdom** – 69 years

Hassanal Bolkiah, **Brunei** – 54 years

Margrethe II, **Denmark** – 49 years

Sultan bin Mohammed Al-Qasimi III,
United Arab Emirates – 49 years

Carl XVI Gustaf, **Sweden** – 48 years

As of November 2021

"I was a queen, and you took away my crown; a wife, and you killed my husband; a mother, and you deprived me of my children. My blood alone remains: take it, but do not make me suffer long."

Marie Antoinette
(1755–1793)

"**A** false report, if believed during three days, may be of great service to a government."

Catherine de' Medici
(1519–1589)

The Worst Queens in History

Catherine the Great, Russia

Mary I, Britain

Marie Antoinette, France

Maria I, Portugal

Empress Irene of Athens, Greece

Catherine de' Medici, France

Ranavalona I, Madagascar

The Shortest-Reigning Monarchs in History

Louis XIX, France – **20 minutes**

Crown Prince Luís Filipe, Portugal – **20 minutes**

Tsar Michael II, Russia – **less than a day**

Queen Jane, England – **9 days**

Napoleon II, France – **16 days**

Taichang, China – **29 days**

Berengaria of Castile, Spain – **2 months, 25 days**

"She [Ranavalona I] was one of the proudest and most cruel women on the face of the earth."

Ida Pfeiffer
(1797–1858)

Biggest Royal Weddings by Cost (Estimated)

1981 – Sheikh Mohammed bin Zayed bin Sultan Al Nahyan & Princess Salama **(£75m+)**

1981 – Prince Charles & Princess Diana **(£57m)**

2011 – Prince Albert & Princess Charlene **(£53m)**

2018 – Prince Harry & Meghan Markle **(£32m)**

2011 – Prince William & Kate Middleton **(£30m)**

Source: hellomagazine.com

"Do we kiss?"

Meghan Markle

The new Duchess of Sussex, questioning her new husband immediately after their wedding

"Yeah!"

Prince Harry

"**O**ne man to live in pleasure and wealth, whiles all other weap and smart for it, that is the part not of a king, but of a jailor."

Sir Thomas More
(1478–1535)

"Commoners"
Who Married Royals

2018 – Meghan Markle & Prince Harry

2018 – Alessandra De Osma & Prince
Christian of Hanover

2015 – Sofia Hellqvist & Prince Carl Philip

2014 – Beatrice Borromeo & Prince
Pierre Casiraghi

2011 – Kate Middleton & Prince William

1956 – Grace Kelly & Prince Rainier III

The richest royal ever is
reputed to be King Bhumibol
Adulyadej, of the Chakri
dynasty of Thailand. He owned
the largest cut diamond in
the world, and had a personal
fortune of £22bn.

Queen Elizabeth II
is a multiple Guinness World
Record holder, including
longest reign, oldest
British monarch, face on the
most currencies (45) and
wealthiest queen.

CHAPTER
FOUR

It's Good *to be* King

For much of history, male monarchs have wielded power. This chapter takes a look at some of the most fascinating, most powerful and most dangerous men ever to wear a crown.

"**G**oodness is something that makes us serene and content; it is magnificent. Those who are not good are evil."

King Bhumibol the Great of Thailand
(1927–2016)

"To be a king is dedication, patience and moderation, self-denial, statesmanship, national unity and, above all, having faith in one's people."

Simeon Saxe-Coburg-Gotha,
politician and former king of Bulgaria
(1937–)

"After long and anxious consideration, I have determined to renounce the throne to which I succeeded on the death of my father, and I am now communicating this, my final and irrevocable decision."

King Edward VIII

(1894–1972)

Abdication letter to Parliament, 1936

"For 24 years my husband has been punished, like a small boy who gets a spanking every day of his life for a small transgression."

Wallace Simpson
(1896–1986)

"It is the King's office to protect and settle the true interpretation of the Law of God within his Dominions."

James I of England and Ireland
(1566–1625)

"A sovereign must constantly heed the will of his people and at the same time care for the poor and humble; he is the servant of the law, and the mainstay of social peace and security."

King Albert I of Belgium
(1875–1934)

"The game's afoot:
Follow your spirit, and upon
this charge
Cry 'God for Harry, England,
and Saint George!'"

William Shakespeare

Henry V, *spoken by King Henry*

"L' etat c'est moi."

["I am the state"]

Louis XIV of France
(1638–1715)

> **"I** devote all my attentions to improving the welfare of my subjects, since I wish to save my soul and go to heaven.**"**

King Charles III of Spain
(1716–1788)

"Deception is the knowledge of kings."

Cardinal Richelieu

(1585–1642)

Maxims, Testament Politique, *1641*

"I think it is a misconception to imagine that the monarchy exists in the interests of the monarch. It doesn't. It exists in the interests of the people.**"**

HRH Prince Philip, Duke of Edinburgh

(1921–2021)

Press conference, Ottawa, 1969

"**M**y grandfather was of peasant stock and I am prouder of that than of my throne. Crowns are lost, but the pure blood of those who have loved the earth does not die."

King Peter I of Serbia
(1844–1921)

"**M**y Lord, if it were not to satisfy the world, and My Realm, I would not do that I must do this day for none earthly thing."

King Henry VIII

To Cromwell on his wedding day to Anne of Cleves

"God, who has given me so many kingdoms to govern, has not given me a son fit to govern them."

King Philip II of Spain
(1527–1598)

"**G**ood jests ought to bite like lambs, not dogs: they should cut, not wound."

King Charles II of England
(1630–1685)

"The king must die so that the country can live."

Maximilien Robespierre,
lawyer and politician during the
French Revolution

(1758–1794)

CHAPTER
FIVE

Queen *of* Hearts

While it is true that many
more men than women have
held power through the
centuries, history has served
up powerful queens and
princesses too...

"I declare before you all that my whole life, whether it be long or short, shall be devoted to your service and the service of our great imperial family to which we all belong."

Queen Elizabeth II
(as Princess Elizabeth)

(1926–)

"Q is for the Queen who, in half a century, hasn't put a foot wrong once. Her accumulated wisdom is extraordinary. Her charm is infinite. She is duty personified."

The Duke of Devonshire

On Queen Elizabeth II

"**F**amily is the most important thing in the world."

Diana, Princess of Wales
(1961–1997)

Queen Elizabeth II, of:

Antigua and Barbuda
Australia
Bahamas
Belize
Canada
Grenada
Jamaica
New Zealand
Papua New Guinea
Saint Kitts and Nevis
Saint Lucia
Saint Vincent and the Grenadines
Solomon Islands
Tuvalu
United Kingdom

"I will do what queens do, I will rule.**"**

Daenerys Targaryen
Game of Thrones

"I say this explicitly, that it is impossible for me to marry. That is the way it is for me. My temper is a mortal enemy to this horrible yoke, which I would not accept, even if I thus would become the ruler of the world."

Christina, Queen of Sweden
(1626–1689)

The Swedish Royal Family
was the first of its kind
to allow female succession,
in 1980.

"I know I have but the body of a weak and feeble woman, but I have the heart and stomach of a king, and of a king of England too."

Queen Elizabeth I

(1533–1603)

The Tilbury Speech, 1588

"The Queen is the only person who can put on a tiara with one hand, while walking downstairs."

Princess Margaret
(1930–2002)

"I have to be seen to be believed."

Queen Elizabeth II
(1926−)

"To be a king and wear a crown is a thing more glorious to them that see it than it is pleasant to them that bear it.**"**

Queen Elizabeth I
(1533–1603)

"Courage! I have shown it for years; think you I shall lose it at the moment when my sufferings are to end?"

Marie Antoinette
(1755–1793)

"**I** owe no allegiance to the provisional government established by a minority of the foreign population .... nor to anyone save the will of my people and the welfare of my country."

Queen Lili'uokalani of the Hawaiian Islands

After the overthrow of the monarchy, 1893

"Those who imagine that a politician would make a better figurehead than a hereditary monarch might perhaps make the acquaintance of more politicians."

Margaret Thatcher
(1925–2013)

By 2016, Queen Elizabeth II had travelled over a million miles on official visits to 117 countries around the world despite not possessing a passport. She has never visited Israel, Greece or Argentina.

"I cannot lead you into battle. I do not give you laws or administer justice but I can do something else — I can give my heart and my devotion to these old islands and to all the peoples of our brotherhood of nations."

Queen Elizabeth II

(1926–)

"**I** am myself a Queen, the daughter of a King, a stranger, and the true Kinswoman of the Queen of England."

Mary, Queen of Scots
(1542–1587)

In every woman there
is a queen. Speak
to the queen and the
queen will answer.

Norwegian Proverb

"I'd like to be a queen in people's hearts but I don't see myself being queen of this country.**"**

Diana, Princess of Wales
(1961–1997)

"Like all best families, we have our share of eccentricities, of impetuous and wayward youngsters and of family disagreements.**"**

Queen Elizabeth II

(1926–)

"I have the heart of a man, not a woman, and I am not afraid of anything.**"**

Queen Elizabeth I
(1533–1603)

The only post-war pop
record in the collection of
Elizabeth the Queen Mother,
when her collection was
made public, was *Graceland* by
Paul Simon.

"**I** do not want a husband who honours me as a queen, if he does not love me as a woman."

Queen Elizabeth I

(1533–1603)

"There are indeed ways for a queen to say what she thinks."

Queen Margrethe II of Denmark
(1940–)

"Great events make me quiet and calm; it is only trifles that irritate my nerves.**"**

Queen Victoria
(1819–1901)

"I have always had the joy of life, uncrushably, a sort of inner sunshine that cannot be put out.**"**

Queen Marie of Romania

"Queen's Counsel, The Joy of Life",
The Birmingham News, *1926*

"Though the sex to which
I belong is considered weak you
will nevertheless find me a rock
that bends to no wind."

Queen Elizabeth I
(1533–1603)

❝If I wore beige, nobody would know who I am.**❞**

Queen Elizabeth II
(1926–)

"**B**ring me a cup of tea and the *Times*."

Queen Victoria
(1819–1901)

"He has, quite simply, been my strength and stay all these years, and I, and his whole family, and this and many other countries, owe him a debt greater than he would ever claim, or we shall ever know."

Queen Elizabeth II

(1926–)

On Prince Philip

127

During World War II,
King George VI held the ranks
of Admiral of the Fleet, Field
Marshal and Marshal of the
Royal Air Force.

At the age of 19, Princess
Elizabeth joined the Auxiliary
Territorial Service. She trained
as a driver and mechanic with
the rank of Second Subaltern.

"**W**hen I am dead and opened, you shall find 'Calais' lying in my heart."

Queen Mary I of England
(1516–1558)

"Queen Salote, whose genial dignity matches her proportions, has won an extraordinary quantity of affection from the British people."

Daily Telegraph

On the Queen of Tonga's visit for the Coronation, 1953

130

"I will remain on the throne until I fall off.**"**

Queen Margrethe II of Denmark
(1940–)

CHAPTER

SIX

Wit &
Wisdom

Throughout the centuries,
all manner of wise words and
witticisms have come
from the mouths of royals, their
subjects and commentators...

"**K**ings are the slaves of history."

Leo Tolstoy

War and Peace, *1869*

"**A** king is sometimes obliged to commit crimes; but they are the crimes of his position."

Emperor Napoleon Bonaparte
(1769–1821)

"**I**t's like chess, you know.
The queen saves the king."

Terry Pratchett

The Shepherd's Crown, *2015*

"A king may be a tool, a thing of straw; but if he serves to frighten our enemies, and secure our property, it is well enough: a scarecrow is a thing of straw, but it protects the corn."

Alexander Pope
(1688–1744)

"**I** have walked into the palaces of kings and queens and into the houses of presidents. And much more. But I could not walk into a hotel in America and get a cup of coffee, and that made me mad."

Josephine Baker
(1906–1975)

"**H**e represented, for us,
a model of character and
deportment for those in high
places. Our respect for him as
an inspirational force was
equalled by our affection for
him as a gentle human being."

General Dwight D Eisenhower
On King George VI, 1952

There is no room for two kings in one castle.

Estonian proverb

"Kings are not born:
they are made by universal
hallucination.**"**

George Bernard Shaw
(1856–1950)

"**K**ings ought to differ from their subjects, not in kind, but in perfection."

Aristotle
(384–322 BCE)

"A king is a king, not because he is rich and powerful, not because he is a successful politician, not because he belongs to a particular creed or to a national group. He is king because he is born."

Jacques Monet
(1930–)

"A king that would not feel his crown too heavy for him, must wear it every day, but if he think it too light, he knoweth not of what metal it is made."

Francis Bacon
(1561–1626)

"That the king can do no wrong is a necessary and fundamental principle of the English constitution."

William Blackstone
Commentaries on the Laws of England, *1765*

"**N**o kingdom can endure two kings."

Agesilaus II, King of Sparta
(Circa 444–360 BCE)

"**A**h! vainest of all things
Is the gratitude of kings."

Henry Wadsworth Longfellow
"Belisarius", 1875

"The state of Monarchy is the supremest thing upon earth; for kings are not only God's lieutenants upon earth and sit upon God's throne, but even by God himself they are called gods."

King James I of England
Speech to Parliament, 1610

An unjust king is like a
river without water

Arabian proverb

"Not all the water in the
rough rude sea
Can wash the balm off from an
anointed king."

William Shakespeare
Richard II

"All kings is mostly rapscallions."

Mark Twain

The Adventures of Huckleberry Finn, *1884*

"**H**istory has remembered the kings and warriors, because they destroyed; art has remembered the people, because they created."

William Morris

The Water of the Wondrous Isles, *1897*

A crown is no cure for
the headache.

Dutch proverb

"**K**ings are like stars —
they rise and set, they have
The worship of the world, but
no repose."

Percy Bysshe Shelley
(1792–1822)

"Fear God. Honour the King."

The Bible

1 Peter 2:17

"**T**hink like a queen.
A queen is not afraid to fail.
Failure is another stepping stone
to greatness."

Oprah Winfrey
(1954–)

"I write by the light of two eternal truths: religion and monarchy, those twin essentials affirmed by contemporary events, and towards which every intelligent author should seek to direct our country."

Honoré de Balzac
(1799–1850)

157

Better a free bird
than a captive king.

Danish proverb

"He is happiest, be he king or peasant, who finds peace in his home."

Johann Wolfgang Von Goethe
(1749–1832)

"If you find someone you love in your life, then hang on to that love.**"**

Diana, Princess of Wales
(1961–1997)

"Everybody must be managed. Queens must be managed. Kings must be managed, for men want managing almost as much as women, and that's saying a good deal."

Thomas Hardy
Under the Greenwood Tree, *1872*

"**G**ive my people plenty of beer, good beer, and cheap beer, and you will have no revolution among them."

Queen Victoria
(1819–1901)

"On the highest throne in the world, we still sit only on our own bottom.**"**

Michel de Montaigne
(1533–1592)

"**M**ost of the mess that is called history comes about because kings and presidents cannot be satisfied with a nice chicken and a good loaf of bread."

Jennifer Donnelly
Revolution, *2010*

The thief who
is not caught is a king.

Indian proverb

"**K**ings also sleep; but the clever ones, with one eye open, just like dolphins and whales."

Mehmet Murat ildan

(1965–)

"I don't think I really came to appreciate what royalty meant to you Brits until I came to Wimbledon, with all its pomp and circumstance. It is tradition, it is such an important factor here and you start thinking it's not bad when you see the effect it has on people.**"**

John McEnroe
The Sunday Telegraph, *2000*

"The important thing is not what they think of me, but what I think of them."

Queen Victoria
(1819–1901)

"What is going to happen to me and all of Russia? I am not prepared to be a Tsar. I never wanted to become one. I know nothing of the business of ruling."

Tsar Nicholas II
_(1868–1918)_

"Through talk, we tamed kings, restrained tyrants, averted revolution."

Tony Benn

Quoted in The Changing Anatomy of Britain
by Anthony Sampson, 1982

"**K**ings are never without flatterers to seduce them, ambition to deprive them, and desires to corrupt them."

Plato

The Republic, *circa 375 BCE*

"**I** was much an enemy to monarchy before I came to Europe. I am ten thousand times more so, since I have seen what they are…

There is scarcely an evil known in these countries, which may not be traced to their king, as its source, nor a good, which is not derived from the small fibres of republicanism existing among them."

Thomas Jefferson

In a letter to George Washington, 1788

It is easy to govern a
kingdom but difficult to
rule your family.

Chinese proverb

"Love and faithfulness keep a king safe; through love his throne is made secure."

The Bible

Proverbs 20:20

"This sleep is sound indeed; this
is a sleep
That from this golden rigol hath
divorc'd
So many English kings."

William Shakespeare

Henry IV, Part 2

"**O**nce a king or queen of Narnia, always a king or queen of Narnia."

C. S. Lewis

The Lion, the Witch and the Wardrobe, *1950*

"For every monarchy overthrown the sky becomes less brilliant, because it loses a star. A republic is ugliness set free."

Anatole France

(1844–1924)

First winner of the Nobel Prize for Literature

"I had been told the Queen is not interested in anything political and speaks only on social issues. On the contrary, the Queen is very well informed on a number of international issues and on security matters."

Vladimir Putin

(1952–)

179

Three are powerful:
the Pope, the king,
and the man who has
nothing.

Italian proverb

"Kings fight for empires,
madmen for applause."

John Dryden
(1631–1700)

"One does not always do the best there is. One does the best one can.**"**

Queen Catherine the Great
(1729–1796)

"Magistrates rule by an established rotation; kings reign for life."

Aristotle
(384–322 BCE)

"**I**n the land of the blind, the one-eyed man is king."

Erasmus

(Attributed)

"I have already joined myself in marriage to a husband, namely the kingdom of England – to Parliament."

Queen Elizabeth I
(1533–1603)

"**Y**esterday we obeyed kings and bent our necks before emperors. But today we kneel only to truth, follow only beauty, and obey only love."

Khalil Gibran

The Vision: Reflections on the Way of the Soul, *1994*

If every fool wore
a crown, we should all
be kings.

Welsh proverb

"Uneasy lies the head that wears a crown."

William Shakespeare

Henry IV, Part 2

"When the Queen says 'well done,' it means so much."

Prince William

(1982–)

"Why do the Gods make kings and queens if not to protect the ones who can't protect themselves?"

George R. R. Martin
A Storm of Swords, *2000*

"A throne is only a bench covered with velvet."

Emperor Napoleon Bonaparte
(1769–1821)

"The Queen's appearances abroad do more in a day to gain goodwill for Britain than all the politicians and diplomats lumped together could achieve in years."

Sir Alec Douglas-Home
_(1903–1995)_